DIRT BIKE CRAZY

KAWASAKI DIRT BIKES

By R. L. Van

WORLD BOOK

BIGFOOT BOOKS

The Quest for Discovery Never Ends

This edition is co-published by agreement between Kaleidoscope and World Book, Inc.

Kaleidoscope Publishing, Inc.
6012 Blue Circle Drive
Minnetonka, MN 55343 U.S.A.

World Book, Inc.
180 North LaSalle St., Suite 900
Chicago IL 60601 U.S.A.

Kaleidoscope ISBNs
978-1-64519-092-9 (library bound)
978-1-64494-153-9 (paperback)
978-1-64519-196-4 (ebook)

World Book ISBN
978-0-7166-4365-4 (library bound)

Library of Congress Control Number
2019939018

Printed in the United States of America.

FIND ME IF YOU CAN!

Bigfoot lurks within one of the images in this book. It's up to you to find him!

TABLE OF
CONTENTS

CHAPTER 1

Team Green

Ryder DiFrancesco is only thirteen. But he's a big name in **motocross**. He's been riding dirt bikes since he was three. And he started racing soon after. He's won Loretta Lynn's three times. Loretta Lynn's is the **Amateur** National Motocross Championship. Ryder was the youngest to win it. He wants to win again.

It's the 2018 Loretta Lynn's championship. Ryder moves his bike to the starting gate. He rides a Kawasaki KX85. It has a lime green fender. A large green plate rises up above it. This connects to the handlebars. He wears a long-sleeved shirt and pants. They are covered in sponsor logos. His helmet is, too.

Ryder DiFrancesco has won at Loretta Lynn's many times.

Ryder is on Team Green. Team Green is Kawasaki's amateur team. It sponsors young motocross riders. Kawasaki gives athletes dirt bikes. It helps them fix their bikes at big races.

The gate drops. Ryder speeds forward. He's in the lead. He makes a sharp turn around the first corner. Then he comes to a series of hills. He jumps over each one. He lands hard. But his KX85 has great **suspension**. There's a spring under his bike's seat. It absorbs the impact when he lands. He can adjust it for the track he's driving.

FUN FACT
Kawasaki started its Team Green program in 1981.

Some parts of the track are wet and muddy. But he can still do great in the mud. He flies through the muddy sections. He does lap after lap. Finally, the end is near. Ryder clears the last hills. He pumps his fist in the air. Zoom! He crosses the finish line. He won the moto! A moto is a race. There's one moto left in the series. He's about to win his fourth national championship.

DiFrancesco rides a KX85. The KX85 is a smaller bike for young riders.

CHAPTER 2

Kawasaki's aerospace division makes planes.

Ships, Trains, and Bikes

Kawasaki didn't always make dirt bikes. It started out building ships. A Japanese man named Shozo Kawasaki started it in 1878. The company grew. It made trains. Wars created demand for Kawasaki's products. The company started building airplanes.

In the 1960s, Kawasaki expanded again. It started making motorcycles. In 1963, it sold its first motocross bike. It was called the B8M. It was based on Kawasaki's B8 street bike. Racers on the B8M raced at a Japanese motocross championship. They won the top six places.

Mia's first bike was a 1969 Kawasaki F21M Green Streak. She loved that bike. It was the first Kawasaki to have lime green paint. She remembered the cushy black seat. It had shining silver fenders. The engine had 28 **horsepower**. That was a lot back then.

It had served her well. But 1988 brought something new. The KX500 was different from the Green Streak. It had blue covers on the **fork**. The fenders were lime green. And it didn't just look different. The engine was larger. It was also more powerful. Mia tightened her helmet strap. It was time to ride the KX500 around the track.

The F21M was a serious racing bike. It came with many spare parts.

PARTS OF A
KAWASAKI KX250

brake lever

number plate

fender

disc brakes

tire

Kawasaki had improved its brakes. Kawasaki was the first major dirt bike company to use disc brakes. Vehicles with disc brakes have metal discs attached to their wheels. A set of brake pads squeezes the discs to slow the vehicle down. Mia could tell the difference. She used to need four fingers to brake. Now, she could pull the lever with one finger. The KX500 was amazing. Mia couldn't wait to find out what else Kawasaki had in store.

Kawasaki continues to improve its bikes.

Kawasaki started making four-stroke bikes in 2004. Four-strokes are heavier than two-strokes. But they're smoother and easier to control. The company keeps making changes. Change is how Kawasaki continues to improve.

CHAPTER 3

Green Machines

Eric had saved up for a new dirt bike. He knew he wanted a Kawasaki. He just wasn't sure which one. He was a motocross racer. But he liked trail riding, too. He was thinking about getting a **street-legal** bike. He wanted to drive it around his city. He went to a dealership. The saleswoman showed him around. She pointed out the KLX250. She told Eric it was a dual-sport bike. It could drive off-road on trails. It was also street legal.

Features like turn signals, headlights, and side mirrors make the KLX250 street legal.

Eric decided to give it a try. He took the KLX250 for a test ride. The seat was high. Fewer obstacles like rocks and logs could reach the engine. Eric pressed the electric start button. This turned the bike on. The engine was quiet. That helped make it street legal. It also had headlights and turn signals.

FUN FACT

Some people call Kawasaki dirt bikes "Kwackers."

The KLX250 is a dual-sport bike, made both for street riding and off-road riding.

The bike felt heavy at first. But it was easy to control. Other dual-sport bikes had more powerful engines. But they were harder to drive. The KLX250 was smooth. Eric drove onto a trail. The bike could climb hills. It could pull through dirt. It wouldn't do well at a motocross track. But it was great for almost everything else.

DIRT BIKE OF CHAMPIONS

Kawasaki bikes win races. KX models have won many AMA National Motocross and Supercross titles. They've won more than any other manufacturer. The bikes win other awards, too. The 2019 KX450 won a big award. It was named *Transworld Motocross*'s "Bike of the Year."

Eric returned to the dealership. He tried out the KX450. This bike was built for motocross. He took it onto the dealer's test track. He could feel the difference immediately. The bike's engine was larger. But the bike was lighter overall. It was the lightest Japanese bike in the 450cc class. He adjusted the handlebars. They could sit in two positions. Eric could adjust other things, too. There were green, black, and white pieces he could attach. These changed the engine's power settings. He put the black one on for the hard-packed track. He also adjusted the fork suspension.

The KX450 is best suited for the motocross track.

The KX450 was also easy to turn. It managed the corners on the track easily. The engine was loud. But it was strong. It powered through the deep dirt on the track. When his test ride was over, Eric had decided. He bought the KX450. But he liked the KLX250, too. He planned to keep saving up. Maybe he could have both someday.

BIKE MODEL	KX250	KX450	KLX250
SUITABLE FOR	Motocross	Motocross	Dual-Sport (Off-road and street)
TRANSMISSION	5-speed	5-speed	6-speed
TYPE OF START	Kick-starter	Electric Starter	Electric Starter
WEIGHT	230 pounds (104 kg)	242 pounds (110 kg)	304 pounds (138 kg)
BASE PRICE	$7,749	$9,299	$5,349

KAWASAKI DIRT BIKES

KX250

KX450

KLX250

CHAPTER 4

Riding to the Podium

Eli Tomac has always been around bikes. His dad raced mountain bikes. But Tomac chose a different kind of bike. He's ridden the old KX450F and new KX450. They've carried him to many victories. He won the Monster Energy Cup in 2018. This is a major supercross event. But Tomac wants to go even further. He wants the 2019 Supercross Championship.

It's March 10, 2019. Tomac straddles his bike. He's at the Daytona International Speedway. The gate drops. He doesn't start with the lead. But he catches up. He sails over hills. Another racer passes him. He sprays dirt back at Tomac. But Tomac won't let that stop him. A series of small hills is next. He flies through on his back wheel. Tomac pulls ahead again! He makes it to the last lap. He soars over the last hill. Tomac crosses the finish line. He gets first place!

There are still more races to go in the series. But Tomac has another win for Kawasaki under his belt. And he has his eyes on the prize.

Eli Tomac competes in supercross. Supercross is done inside stadiums.

FUN FACT

Tomac also won the Monster Energy Cup in 2016.

Meg Rutledge has ridden dirt bikes since she was three years old.

Kawasaki supports riders on other continents, too. Motocross racer Meg Rutledge is making a name for herself in Australia. Meg Rutledge started racing at seven years old. She became the 2018 Australian Women's **Supermoto** champion. She was twenty-three. She and her KX250 were having an excellent year. This was her fourth championship title in 2018.

Rutledge decided to enter a new contest. It was the FIM Oceania Supermoto Championship. She faced off against all men. They rode 450cc bikes. Their bikes were more powerful than her 250cc bike. She'd never competed in that style of supermoto. Rutledge didn't win. But she was a strong competitor. Rutledge dreams of becoming world champion one day.

Kawasaki has a long history of building champions.
Its Team Green program helps young riders prepare
for motocross careers. Its bikes have won huge titles.

Kawasaki is a brand
for champions.

And riders like Tomac and Rutledge keep Kawasaki on championship podiums.

BEYOND
THE BOOK

After reading the book, it's time to think about what you learned. Try the following exercises to jumpstart your ideas.

THINK

DIFFERENT SOURCES. Think about what types of sources you could find on the AMA Amateur National Motocross Championship (often called Loretta Lynn's). What could you find in a news article? What could you learn at a motocross track? How could each of the sources be useful in its own way?

CREATE

PRIMARY SOURCES. A primary source is an original document, photograph, or interview. Make a list of different primary sources you might be able to find about Kawasaki dirt bikes. What new information might you learn from these sources?

SHARE

SUM IT UP. Write one paragraph summarizing the important points from this book. Make sure it's in your own words. Don't just copy what is in the text. Share the paragraph with a classmate. Does your classmate have any comments about the summary? Do they have additional questions about Kawasaki dirt bikes?

GROW

DRAWING CONNECTIONS. Create a drawing that shows the connection between Kawasaki dirt bikes and motocross athletes. How does learning about motocross athletes help you to better understand Kawasaki dirt bikes?

RESEARCH NINJA

Visit *www.ninjaresearcher.com/0929* to learn how
to take your research skills and book report writing to the next level!

RESEARCH

DIGITAL LITERACY TOOLS

SEARCH LIKE A PRO
Learn about how to use search engines to find useful websites.

FACT OR FAKE?
Discover how you can tell a trusted website from an untrustworthy resource.

TEXT DETECTIVE
Explore how to zero in on the information you need most.

SHOW YOUR WORK
Research responsibly—learn how to cite sources.

WRITE

GET TO THE POINT
Learn how to express your main ideas.

PLAN OF ATTACK
Learn prewriting exercises and create an outline.

DOWNLOADABLE REPORT FORMS

Further Resources

BOOKS

Murray, Julie. *Kawasaki*. Abdo Publishing, 2019.

Polydoros, Lori. *Dirt Bike Racing*. Capstone, 2014.

Shaffer, Lindsay. *Dirt Bikes.* Bellwether Media, 2019.

WEBSITES

FACTSURFER

Factsurfer.com gives you a safe, fun way to find more information.

1. Go to www.factsurfer.com.

2. Enter "Kawasaki Dirt Bikes" into the search box and click 🔍.

3. Select your book cover to see a list of related websites.

Glossary

amateur: An amateur athlete doesn't get paid for competing. Kawasaki's Team Green is an amateur racing team.

fork: The fork of a bike or motorcycle connects the front wheel to the frame and provides suspension. The 2019 KX models have springs inside the fork to absorb shock.

horsepower: One horsepower is the power it takes to lift 550 pounds one foot in one second. The KX450 can generate more than 50 horsepower.

motocross: Motocross is a sport that takes place on rough outdoor dirt courses that are built into the natural land. Motocross tracks feature jumps, hills, and other obstacles.

street-legal: A street-legal vehicle has the necessary features and adjustments to make it safe to drive on public roads. The street-legal KLX250 has a headlight, turn signals, and a quiet engine.

supercross: Supercross is a version of motocross that takes place inside stadiums on man-made dirt courses. Eli Tomac wanted to win the 2019 Monster Energy Supercross championship.

supermoto: Supermoto is a type of modified dirt bike racing that takes place on courses that combine motocross, road, and flat-track styles. Meg Rutledge was the 2018 Australian Women's Supermoto champion.

suspension: A vehicle's suspension absorbs shock and keeps riders comfortable over rough courses. Kawasaki updated its bikes' rear suspension so the back of the bike would absorb more shock.

Index

PHOTO CREDITS

The images in this book are reproduced through the courtesy of: Vytautas Kielaitis/Shutterstock Images, front cover; Kawasaki Media, pp. 3, 4, 4–5, 6–7, 10, 11, 12–13, 13, 14–15, 16–17, 18, 18–19, 21 (top), 21 (middle), 21 (bottom), 23, 25, 26–27, 30; viper-zero/Shutterstock Images, pp. 8–9; Red Line Editorial, pp. 20–21; Gaetano Piazzolla/Actionplus/Newscom, p. 24.

ABOUT THE AUTHOR

R. L. Van is a writer and editor from Minnesota. She loves books, animals, and crossword puzzles.